What Is a Solstice?

by Gail Terp

childsworld.com

Published by The Child's World®
1980 Lookout Drive • Mankato, MN 56003-1705
800-599-READ • www.childsworld.com

Acknowledgments
The Child's World®: Mary Swensen, Publishing Director
Red Line Editorial: Editorial direction and production
The Design Lab: Design

Photographs ©: Chaikovskiy Igor/Shutterstock Images, cover,
1; Shutterstock Images, 5, 11, 17; Red Line Editorial, 7; Yuriy Kulik/
Shutterstock Images, 9; Holly Kuchera/Shutterstock Images,
13; Ildi Papp/Shutterstock Images, 14; Dudarev Mikhail/
Shutterstock Images, 19; Catalin Petolea/Shutterstock, 20

ISBN 9781503807921
LCCN 2015958189

Printed in the United States of America
Mankato, MN
June, 2016
PA02299

ABOUT THE AUTHOR

Gail Terp is a retired elementary teacher who now writes for kids and beginning adult readers. She lives in Hudson Falls, New York.

TABLE of CONTENTS

CHAPTER 1

What Makes the Seasons?

Did you know Earth moves? You can't feel it, but it does. Earth rotates. This means it spins. It spins and never stops. Imagine a long pole sticking through Earth. This pretend pole is Earth's **axis**. Earth rotates on it. It turns like a spinning top.

Rotating makes daytime and nighttime. Each day of the week has 24 hours. Earth makes one full turn around its axis from Monday to Tuesday. The part of Earth that faces the sun has daylight. The part that faces away has night.

The sun is a star. At night, you can see many other stars that are very far away from Earth.

Earth moves another way, too. It **orbits** the sun. That means it travels around it. Each orbit takes about 365 days. This is one year.

Imagine a line around Earth. It circles around Earth's middle. This line is the **equator**. It splits Earth into two halves. Each half is a **hemisphere**. The northern hemisphere is the top half. The southern hemisphere is the bottom half.

As Earth orbits the sun, it tilts. The tilt makes the seasons. The northern hemisphere is tilted toward the sun for part of the year. It is summer in the north then. When the northern hemisphere is tilted away, it is winter there.

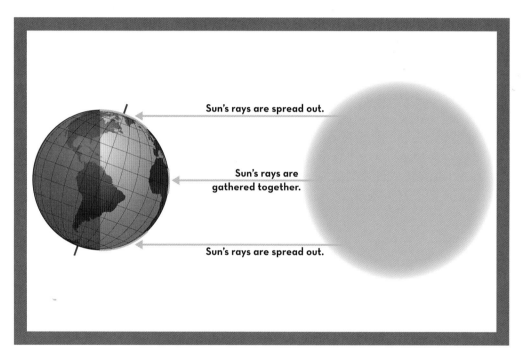

In summer, the sun's rays are more direct. They feel more powerful.

CHAPTER 2

What Is a Winter Solstice?

What happens in winter? Some places get a little bit of snow. And some places get a lot of it! But for most places, it means the weather gets colder.

The sun still shines in winter. It still gives us heat and light. So why does it get colder? Remember that Earth rotates on its axis. But the axis is not straight up and down. It is tilted. As Earth orbits, part of it is tilted away from the sun. The sun's rays hit Earth at an angle. They are spread out. This means the heat and light we get from the sun are spread out, too.

The sun ray's hit Earth at different angles from summer to winter.

The land does not get as warm. The weather gets colder. It makes winter.

What else happens in winter? For most places, the days get shorter. There are fewer hours when the sun is shining. This is also caused by the tilt of Earth's axis. The hemisphere that is tilted away from the sun gets less sunlight. It spends more time out of reach from the sun's rays. This means the sun rises later in the day. The sun sets earlier, too. In most places, there are fewer than 12 hours of daylight in winter.

Plants **react** to winter. They start changing when weather gets colder.

The shorter days cause changes, too. Plants can't get as much energy from the sun. Some plants die. Others rest. Their leaves die. But the roots stay safe underground.

Animals react to winter. Some move to a warmer place. This is called migration. Some animals adapt. Wolves grow a thicker coat of fur to help keep them warm. Fish stay alive by going **dormant**. Their bodies slow down. They breathe less often. They use only a tiny bit of energy.

You can feel it when the weather starts getting colder. You might notice

Without a thick coat of fur, wolves would freeze in winter.

the sun setting earlier in the day. But how do you know when winter really starts? It starts on the shortest day of the year. This is called the winter solstice.

In the southern hemisphere, it is the opposite. December 21 is usually the summer solstice.

That day is usually December 21 in the northern hemisphere.

But sometimes it is on December 22 instead. Why? Earth's orbit around the sun takes a little longer than 365 days. It takes about six more hours than a full year. So what happens to this extra time? Every four years, an extra day is added to the calendar. This is called a leap year. There are 366 days during those years. This extra time is also why the winter solstice is not always on December 21 in the northern hemisphere.

CHAPTER 3

What Is a Summer Solstice?

How is summer different than winter? The weather gets warmer. Part of Earth is tilted toward the sun. The sun's rays are not at such an angle anymore. They are not so spread out. That makes the sunlight strong. It heats the air. It heats the land. This gives us warm weather. It gives us summer.

In summer, the days are longer. The hemisphere that is tilted toward the sun gets more sunlight. The sun rises early in the morning. It also sets late in the day.

Norway is far from the equator. Summer
nights do not last long there.

Nighttime does not last as long. Some places have only a few hours of darkness.

The longer days and stronger sunlight help plants grow well. They can make more energy. Their roots spread in the warm dirt. Their leaves grow in the bright sun.

What happens to the animals that adapted to the winter weather? They adapt to summer, too. Wolves shed their thicker coats. Thinner coats are all they need in the warm weather. Fish are no longer dormant. The ice melts. The fish can breathe more often. They have more food to eat.

In summer, fish can breathe more often. There is no more ice covering the water.

You can feel the sun's rays getting stronger. You might notice the sun setting later in the evening. But when does

The sun sets late on the summer solstice.

summer really start? The longest day in the northern hemisphere is usually June 21. This is the summer solstice.

Earth rotates on its axis. The axis is tilted. Earth also orbits the sun. Sometimes part of Earth is tilted away from the sun. This makes the sunlight weaker. The days are shorter. The shortest day is called the winter solstice. Sometimes part of Earth is tilted toward the sun. The sunlight is stronger. The days get longer. The longest day is called the summer solstice.

Changes in Sunlight

See how sunlight changes from one solstice to another!

What You Need
2 pieces of paper
pencil
2 teaspoons of paint
paintbrush

What to Do
1. Draw a small circle on one sheet of paper. Spread exactly one teaspoon of paint on this circle using the paintbrush.
2. Draw a circle twice as big on the other sheet of paper. Spread the other teaspoon of paint on this circle.
3. Compare the two circles. Notice that the color on the first sheet of paper looks brighter. This is like the sun's rays in summer. The color on the second circle looks weaker. This is like the sun's rays in winter.

Glossary

axis (AK-sis) An axis is a real or imaginary line through the center of something, which an object spins around. Earth rotates around its axis once each day.

dormant (DORM-uhnt) Something that is dormant is not active for a time. Fish are dormant in winter to survive the cold weather.

equator (i-KWAY-tur) The equator is an imaginary line around the middle of Earth that is equal distance from the North and South Poles. The equator splits Earth into two halves.

hemisphere (HEM-i-sfeer) A hemisphere is one half of Earth. Earth is divided into the northern hemisphere and the southern hemisphere.

orbits (OR-bits) When an object orbits, it moves in a circle around something else. Earth orbits around the sun in about 365 days.

react (ree-AKT) To react means to respond to someone or something. An animal can react to cold weather by growing a thicker coat.

To Learn More

In the Library

Amoroso, Cynthia, and Robert B. Noyed. *Summer*. Mankato, MN: The Child's World, 2014.

Dawson, Emily C. *Summer and Winter*. Mankato, MN: Amicus, 2012.

Orr, Tamra B. *Tell Me Why It Snows*. Ann Arbor, MI: Cherry Lake Publishing, 2015.

On the Web

Visit our Web site for links about Earth's solstices:
childsworld.com/links

Note to Parents, Teachers, and Librarians: We routinely verify our Web links to make sure they are safe and active sites. So encourage your readers to check them out!

Index